2020 Debt Tracker

Financial Goals

Next 6-12 months	It Will Cost	Budget Per Month
1.		
2.		
3.		
4.		
5.		
6.		

Next 1-2 Years	It Will Cost	Budget Per Month
1.		
2.		
3.		
4.		
5.		
6.		

Next 6-12 months	It Will Cost	Budget Per Month
1.		
2.		
3.		
4.		
5.		
6.		

Yearly Sinking Funds and Memberships

Description	Due Date	Yearly Cost	$ per month

Get Out Of Debt List

Creditor	Interest	Min Payment	Balance	Due Date

Savings

Account	Previous Balance	Deposit	New Balance

January

			1	2	3	4
5	6	7	8	9	10	11
12	13	14	15	16	17	18
19	20	21	22	23	24	25
26	27	28	29	30	31	

Bi-Weekly Bills/Expenses Snapshot

Paycheck 1:	
Other Income:	
Total Income:	

Expense	Amount	Due Date	Paid Y/N

TOTAL INCOME:	
TOTAL EXPENSES:	
BALANCE	

Expense Tracker

Date	Description	Category	Deposit	Withdraw	Balance

Expense Tracker

Date	Description	Category	Deposit	Withdraw	Balance

Expense Tracker

Date	Description	Category	Deposit	Withdraw	Balance

Bi-Weekly Bills/Expenses Snapshot

Paycheck 2:	
Other Income:	
Total Income:	

Expense	Amount	Due Date	Paid Y/N

TOTAL INCOME:	
TOTAL EXPENSES:	
BALANCE	

Expense Tracker

Date	Description	Category	Deposit	Withdraw	Balance

Expense Tracker

Date	Description	Category	Deposit	Withdraw	Balance

Expense Tracker

Date	Description	Category	Deposit	Withdraw	Balance

Sinking Funds

Type	Deposit	Withdraw	Balance

Savings

Type	Deposit	Withdraw	Balance

Monthly Debt Payoff Tracker

Account	Beg Balance	Min Payment	Extra Payment	New Balance

Total Debt Balance	
Last Month Balance	
This Month Balance	

FEBRUARY

						1
2	3	4	5	6	7	8
9	10	11	12	13	14	15
16	17	18	19	20	21	22
23	24	25	26	27	28	29

Bi-Weekly Bills/Expenses Snapshot

Paycheck 1:	
Other Income:	
Total Income:	

Expense	Amount	Due Date	Paid Y/N

TOTAL INCOME:	
TOTAL EXPENSES:	
BALANCE	

Expense Tracker

Date	Description	Category	Deposit	Withdraw	Balance

Expense Tracker

Date	Description	Category	Deposit	Withdraw	Balance

Expense Tracker

Date	Description	Category	Deposit	Withdraw	Balance

Bi-Weekly Bills/Expenses Snapshot

Paycheck 2:	
Other Income:	
Total Income:	

Expense	Amount	Due Date	Paid Y/N

TOTAL INCOME:	
TOTAL EXPENSES:	
BALANCE	

Expense Tracker

Date	Description	Category	Deposit	Withdraw	Balance

Expense Tracker

Date	Description	Category	Deposit	Withdraw	Balance

Expense Tracker

Date	Description	Category	Deposit	Withdraw	Balance

Sinking Funds

Type	Deposit	Withdraw	Balance

Savings

Type	Deposit	Withdraw	Balance

Monthly Debt Payoff Tracker

Account	Beg Balance	Min Payment	Extra Payment	New Balance

Total Debt Balance	
Last Month Balance	
This Month Balance	

MARCH

1	2	3	4	5	6	7
8	9	10	11	12	13	14
15	16	17	18	19	20	21
22	23	24	25	26	27	28
29	30	31				

Bi-Weekly Bills/Expenses Snapshot

Paycheck 1:	
Other Income:	
Total Income:	

Expense	Amount	Due Date	Paid Y/N

TOTAL INCOME:	
TOTAL EXPENSES:	
BALANCE	

Expense Tracker

Date	Description	Category	Deposit	Withdraw	Balance

Expense Tracker

Date	Description	Category	Deposit	Withdraw	Balance

Expense Tracker

Date	Description	Category	Deposit	Withdraw	Balance

Bi-Weekly Bills/Expenses Snapshot

Paycheck 2:	
Other Income:	
Total Income:	

Expense	Amount	Due Date	Paid Y/N

TOTAL INCOME:	
TOTAL EXPENSES:	
BALANCE	

Expense Tracker

Date	Description	Category	Deposit	Withdraw	Balance

Expense Tracker

Date	Description	Category	Deposit	Withdraw	Balance

Expense Tracker

Date	Description	Category	Deposit	Withdraw	Balance

Sinking Funds

Type	Deposit	Withdraw	Balance

Savings

Type	Deposit	Withdraw	Balance

Monthly Debt Payoff Tracker

Account	Beg Balance	Min Payment	Extra Payment	New Balance

Total Debt Balance	
Last Month Balance	
This Month Balance	

APRIL

			1	2	3	4
5	6	7	8	9	10	11
12	13	14	15	16	17	18
19	20	21	22	23	24	25
26	27	28	29	30		

....

....

....

....

....

....

....

....

....

Bi-Weekly Bills/Expenses Snapshot

Paycheck 1:	
Other Income:	
Total Income:	

Expense	Amount	Due Date	Paid Y/N

TOTAL INCOME:	
TOTAL EXPENSES:	
BALANCE	

Expense Tracker

Date	Description	Category	Deposit	Withdraw	Balance

Expense Tracker

Date	Description	Category	Deposit	Withdraw	Balance

Expense Tracker

Date	Description	Category	Deposit	Withdraw	Balance

Bi-Weekly Bills/Expenses Snapshot

Paycheck 2:	
Other Income:	
Total Income:	

Expense	Amount	Due Date	Paid Y/N

TOTAL INCOME:	
TOTAL EXPENSES:	
BALANCE	

Expense Tracker

Date	Description	Category	Deposit	Withdraw	Balance

Expense Tracker

Date	Description	Category	Deposit	Withdraw	Balance

Expense Tracker

Date	Description	Category	Deposit	Withdraw	Balance

Sinking Funds

Type	Deposit	Withdraw	Balance

Savings

Type	Deposit	Withdraw	Balance

Monthly Debt Payoff Tracker

Account	Beg Balance	Min Payment	Extra Payment	New Balance

Total Debt Balance	
Last Month Balance	
This Month Balance	

MAY

					1	2
3	4	5	6	7	8	9
10	11	12	13	14	15	16
17	18	19	20	21	22	23
24	25	26	27	28	29	30
31						

Bi-Weekly Bills/Expenses Snapshot

Paycheck 1:	
Other Income:	
Total Income:	

Expense	Amount	Due Date	Paid Y/N

TOTAL INCOME:	
TOTAL EXPENSES:	
BALANCE	

Expense Tracker

Date	Description	Category	Deposit	Withdraw	Balance

Expense Tracker

Date	Description	Category	Deposit	Withdraw	Balance

Expense Tracker

Date	Description	Category	Deposit	Withdraw	Balance

Bi-Weekly Bills/Expenses Snapshot

Paycheck 2:	
Other Income:	
Total Income:	

Expense	Amount	Due Date	Paid Y/N

TOTAL INCOME:	
TOTAL EXPENSES:	
BALANCE	

Expense Tracker

Date	Description	Category	Deposit	Withdraw	Balance

Expense Tracker

Date	Description	Category	Deposit	Withdraw	Balance

Expense Tracker

Date	Description	Category	Deposit	Withdraw	Balance

Sinking Funds

Type	Deposit	Withdraw	Balance

Savings

Type	Deposit	Withdraw	Balance

Monthly Debt Payoff Tracker

Account	Beg Balance	Min Payment	Extra Payment	New Balance

Total Debt Balance	
Last Month Balance	
This Month Balance	

JUNE

	1	2	3	4	5	6
7	8	9	10	11	12	13
14	15	16	17	18	19	20
21	22	23	24	25	26	27
28	29	30				

Bi-Weekly Bills/Expenses Snapshot

Paycheck 1:	
Other Income:	
Total Income:	

Expense	Amount	Due Date	Paid Y/N

TOTAL INCOME:	
TOTAL EXPENSES:	
BALANCE	

Expense Tracker

Date	Description	Category	Deposit	Withdraw	Balance

Expense Tracker

Date	Description	Category	Deposit	Withdraw	Balance

Expense Tracker

Date	Description	Category	Deposit	Withdraw	Balance

Bi-Weekly Bills/Expenses Snapshot

Paycheck 2:	
Other Income:	
Total Income:	

Expense	Amount	Due Date	Paid Y/N

TOTAL INCOME:	
TOTAL EXPENSES:	
BALANCE	

Expense Tracker

Date	Description	Category	Deposit	Withdraw	Balance

Expense Tracker

Date	Description	Category	Deposit	Withdraw	Balance

Expense Tracker

Date	Description	Category	Deposit	Withdraw	Balance

Sinking Funds

Type	Deposit	Withdraw	Balance

Savings

Type	Deposit	Withdraw	Balance

Monthly Debt Payoff Tracker

Account	Beg Balance	Min Payment	Extra Payment	New Balance

Total Debt Balance	
Last Month Balance	
This Month Balance	

JULY

			1	2	3	4
5	6	7	8	9	10	11
12	13	14	15	16	17	18
19	20	21	22	23	24	25
26	27	28	29	30	31	

Bi-Weekly Bills/Expenses Snapshot

Paycheck 1:	
Other Income:	
Total Income:	

Expense	Amount	Due Date	Paid Y/N

TOTAL INCOME:	
TOTAL EXPENSES:	
BALANCE	

Expense Tracker

Date	Description	Category	Deposit	Withdraw	Balance

Expense Tracker

Date	Description	Category	Deposit	Withdraw	Balance

Expense Tracker

Date	Description	Category	Deposit	Withdraw	Balance

Bi-Weekly Bills/Expenses Snapshot

Paycheck 2:	
Other Income:	
Total Income:	

Expense	Amount	Due Date	Paid Y/N

TOTAL INCOME:	
TOTAL EXPENSES:	
BALANCE	

Expense Tracker

Date	Description	Category	Deposit	Withdraw	Balance

Expense Tracker

Date	Description	Category	Deposit	Withdraw	Balance

Expense Tracker

Date	Description	Category	Deposit	Withdraw	Balance

Sinking Funds

Type	Deposit	Withdraw	Balance

Savings

Type	Deposit	Withdraw	Balance

Monthly Debt Payoff Tracker

Account	Beg Balance	Min Payment	Extra Payment	New Balance

Total Debt Balance	
Last Month Balance	
This Month Balance	

AUGUST

						1
2	3	4	5	6	7	8
9	10	11	12	13	14	15
16	17	18	19	20	21	22
23	24	25	26	27	28	29
30	31					

Bi-Weekly Bills/Expenses Snapshot

Paycheck 1:	
Other Income:	
Total Income:	

Expense	Amount	Due Date	Paid Y/N

TOTAL INCOME:	
TOTAL EXPENSES:	
BALANCE	

Expense Tracker

Date	Description	Category	Deposit	Withdraw	Balance

Expense Tracker

Date	Description	Category	Deposit	Withdraw	Balance

Expense Tracker

Date	Description	Category	Deposit	Withdraw	Balance

Bi-Weekly Bills/Expenses Snapshot

Paycheck 2:	
Other Income:	
Total Income:	

Expense	Amount	Due Date	Paid Y/N

TOTAL INCOME:	
TOTAL EXPENSES:	
BALANCE	

Expense Tracker

Date	Description	Category	Deposit	Withdraw	Balance

Expense Tracker

Date	Description	Category	Deposit	Withdraw	Balance

Expense Tracker

Date	Description	Category	Deposit	Withdraw	Balance

Bi-Weekly Bills/Expenses Snapshot

Paycheck 2:	
Other Income:	
Total Income:	

Expense	Amount	Due Date	Paid Y/N

TOTAL INCOME:	
TOTAL EXPENSES:	
BALANCE	

Sinking Funds

Type	Deposit	Withdraw	Balance

Savings

Type	Deposit	Withdraw	Balance

Monthly Debt Payoff Tracker

Account	Beg Balance	Min Payment	Extra Payment	New Balance

Total Debt Balance	
Last Month Balance	
This Month Balance	

SEPTEMBER

		1	2	3	4	5
6	7	8	9	10	11	12
13	14	15	16	17	18	19
20	21	22	23	24	25	26
27	28	19	30			

Bi-Weekly Bills/Expenses Snapshot

Paycheck 1:	
Other Income:	
Total Income:	

Expense	Amount	Due Date	Paid Y/N

TOTAL INCOME:	
TOTAL EXPENSES:	
BALANCE	

Expense Tracker

Date	Description	Category	Deposit	Withdraw	Balance

Expense Tracker

Date	Description	Category	Deposit	Withdraw	Balance

Expense Tracker

Date	Description	Category	Deposit	Withdraw	Balance

Bi-Weekly Bills/Expenses Snapshot

Paycheck 2:	
Other Income:	
Total Income:	

Expense	Amount	Due Date	Paid Y/N

TOTAL INCOME:	
TOTAL EXPENSES:	
BALANCE	

Expense Tracker

Date	Description	Category	Deposit	Withdraw	Balance

Expense Tracker

Date	Description	Category	Deposit	Withdraw	Balance

Expense Tracker

Date	Description	Category	Deposit	Withdraw	Balance

Sinking Funds

Type	Deposit	Withdraw	Balance

Savings

Type	Deposit	Withdraw	Balance

Monthly Debt Payoff Tracker

Account	Beg Balance	Min Payment	Extra Payment	New Balance

Total Debt Balance	
Last Month Balance	
This Month Balance	

OCTOBER

				1	2	3
4	5	6	7	8	9	10
11	12	13	14	15	16	17
18	19	20	21	22	23	24
25	16	27	28	29	30	31

Bi-Weekly Bills/Expenses Snapshot

Paycheck 1:	
Other Income:	
Total Income:	

Expense	Amount	Due Date	Paid Y/N

TOTAL INCOME:	
TOTAL EXPENSES:	
BALANCE	

Expense Tracker

Date	Description	Category	Deposit	Withdraw	Balance

Expense Tracker

Date	Description	Category	Deposit	Withdraw	Balance

Expense Tracker

Date	Description	Category	Deposit	Withdraw	Balance

Bi-Weekly Bills/Expenses Snapshot

Paycheck 2:	
Other Income:	
Total Income:	

Expense	Amount	Due Date	Paid Y/N

TOTAL INCOME:	
TOTAL EXPENSES:	
BALANCE	

Expense Tracker

Date	Description	Category	Deposit	Withdraw	Balance

Expense Tracker

Date	Description	Category	Deposit	Withdraw	Balance

Expense Tracker

Date	Description	Category	Deposit	Withdraw	Balance

Sinking Funds

Type	Deposit	Withdraw	Balance

Savings

Type	Deposit	Withdraw	Balance

Monthly Debt Payoff Tracker

Account	Beg Balance	Min Payment	Extra Payment	New Balance

Total Debt Balance	
Last Month Balance	
This Month Balance	

NOVEMBER

1	2	3	4	5	6	7
8	9	10	11	12	13	14
15	16	17	18	19	20	21
22	23	24	25	26	27	28
29	30					

Bi-Weekly Bills/Expenses Snapshot

Paycheck 1:	
Other Income:	
Total Income:	

Expense	Amount	Due Date	Paid Y/N

TOTAL INCOME:	
TOTAL EXPENSES:	
BALANCE	

Expense Tracker

Date	Description	Category	Deposit	Withdraw	Balance

Expense Tracker

Date	Description	Category	Deposit	Withdraw	Balance

Expense Tracker

Date	Description	Category	Deposit	Withdraw	Balance

Bi-Weekly Bills/Expenses Snapshot

Paycheck 2:	
Other Income:	
Total Income:	

Expense	Amount	Due Date	Paid Y/N

TOTAL INCOME:	
TOTAL EXPENSES:	
BALANCE	

Expense Tracker

Date	Description	Category	Deposit	Withdraw	Balance

Expense Tracker

Date	Description	Category	Deposit	Withdraw	Balance

Expense Tracker

Date	Description	Category	Deposit	Withdraw	Balance

Sinking Funds

Type	Deposit	Withdraw	Balance

Savings

Type	Deposit	Withdraw	Balance

Monthly Debt Payoff Tracker

Account	Beg Balance	Min Payment	Extra Payment	New Balance

Total Debt Balance	
Last Month Balance	
This Month Balance	

DECEMBER

		1	2	3	4	5
6	7	8	9	10	11	12
13	14	15	16	17	18	19
20	21	22	23	24	25	26
27	28	29	30	31		

....

....

....

....

....

....

....

....

....

Bi-Weekly Bills/Expenses Snapshot

Paycheck 1:	
Other Income:	
Total Income:	

Expense	Amount	Due Date	Paid Y/N

TOTAL INCOME:	
TOTAL EXPENSES:	
BALANCE	

Expense Tracker

Date	Description	Category	Deposit	Withdraw	Balance

Expense Tracker

Date	Description	Category	Deposit	Withdraw	Balance

Expense Tracker

Date	Description	Category	Deposit	Withdraw	Balance

Bi-Weekly Bills/Expenses Snapshot

Paycheck 2:	
Other Income:	
Total Income:	

Expense	Amount	Due Date	Paid Y/N

TOTAL INCOME:	
TOTAL EXPENSES:	
BALANCE	

Expense Tracker

Date	Description	Category	Deposit	Withdraw	Balance

Expense Tracker

Date	Description	Category	Deposit	Withdraw	Balance

Expense Tracker

Date	Description	Category	Deposit	Withdraw	Balance

Sinking Funds

Type	Deposit	Withdraw	Balance

Savings

Type	Deposit	Withdraw	Balance

Monthly Debt Payoff Tracker

Account	Beg Balance	Min Payment	Extra Payment	New Balance

Total Debt Balance	
Last Month Balance	
This Month Balance	